FROM THE DEPTHS TO THE HEIGHTS

A Biblical Perspective on Depression

Cleon Alleyne

From the Depths to the Heights: A Biblical Perspective on Depression

Scripture References

Unless otherwise noted, all Scripture quotations in this publication are taken from the **New International Version (NIV)** of the Bible, 2011 edition.

DEDICATION

To everyone battling the heavy burden of depression, This book is for you.

In the moments when the darkness feels overwhelming and the weight seems too much to bear, know that you are not alone. Your struggles do not define you, and even in the deepest valleys, there is hope.

May these pages remind you that your journey is seen, your pain is real, and there is a God who walks beside you through it all. You are loved, you are valuable, and you are never forgotten.

Together, we will rise from the depths to the heights.

ACKNOWLEDGMENTS

I want to take a moment to express my heartfelt gratitude to those who have been a source of strength and support throughout my journey with depression. My worst moments unfolded here in Finland, a period when I often felt overwhelmed and isolated. Yet, even in the depths of despair, I discovered incredible resources in this country that have been vital to my healing.

I am profoundly grateful for my therapist, whose wisdom and compassion have guided me through the complexities of my emotions. The support of my church community has also been invaluable, providing a deep sense of belonging and encouragement during difficult times. To my family and friends, thank you for your unwavering support. Although I isolated myself from many during this challenging period, some faithful friends stood by me.

While I will not name you, your presence and encouragement have meant the world to me, reminding me that I was not alone in my struggles. This book is not just a reflection of my journey; it is a testament to the love and support I received from all of you. Thank you for being part of my story and for helping me rise from the depths to the heights of faith and hope.

TABLE OF CONTENTS

DEDICATION iii

ACKNOWLEDGMENTS... v

INTRODUCTION 1

CHAPTER 1: UNDERSTANDING DEPRESSION 4

CHAPTER 27: Biblical Perspectives on Depression................ 7

CHAPTER 3: Trials and Suffering 10

CHAPTER 4: God's Presence in Darkness............................ 14

CHAPTER 5: The Role of Faith in Healing.......................... 18

CHAPTER 6: The Comfort of the Holy Spirit...................... 22

CHAPTER 7: Building a Supportive Community.................. 26

CHAPTER 8: Finding Hope in Scripture............................. 29

CHAPTER 9: Practical Steps Toward Healing 32

CHAPTER10: Wrestling with Darkness............................ 36

CHAPTER 11: Hope in the Valley 42

CHAPTER 12: Celebrating God's Faithfulness 53

CONCLUSION.. 64

INDEX 65

CALL TO ACTION 68

INTRODUCTION

epression is a deeply personal and often isolating experience, one that many people face yet rarely speak of, especially within faith communities. For years, I found myself caught in that silence, navigating the darkness alone. As a missionary pastor, I was well-versed in teaching about hope and resilience, but when depression crept into my own life, it challenged my beliefs and my understanding of what it meant to trust God through suffering. This book is born out of that journey—an attempt to bring light to the shadows of depression through the lens of Scripture and personal experience.

My story is one of faith tested by fire. Like many, I've experienced moments of profound loss, deep despair, and a seemingly relentless search for hope. These trials forced me to confront the reality of depression, not as something foreign, but as a companion on my path—a burden I carried even as I sought to uplift others. In those moments of quiet struggle, I realized how little we talk about depression in our faith circles, and how much we need to.

Through this book, I seek to open a long-overdue conversation. Depression is not a sign of weak faith, nor does it disqualify us from the love and grace of God. In fact, some of the greatest figures in the Bible—David, Elijah, and Job—wrestled with deep sorrow, and it was in their vulnerability that they discovered God's profound presence and strength. The Bible speaks to our pain, our questions, and our need for healing, offering a roadmap for navigating these difficult emotions.

But this book is more than just my story. It's about the countless others who, like me, have found themselves grappling with depression, unsure where to turn. In sharing my journey, I hope to offer not only a sense of solidarity but also biblical insights and practical advice that can help guide others toward hope and healing. Depression, I've learned, is not just an individual battle; it is a shared human experience that connects us all. We may carry it in silence, but we do not carry it alone.

Throughout these pages, I invite you to walk with me as we explore how faith and depression can coexist. We'll look at the Scriptures that speak to our struggles, the promises of God that give us strength, and the power of vulnerability that helps us heal. Together, we'll break down the walls of stigma and shame that so often surround mental health within faith communities.

This book blends biblical truths with personal stories, not only my own but also those of others who have found themselves in the depths of despair. It is a journey of reflection, healing, and, ultimately, rising. I hope that, through these reflections, you will find encouragement and comfort, knowing that depression is not the end of your story. There is hope in God's love, and there is healing to be found, both in Scripture and the community around you.

As we embark on this journey together, I invite you to bring your own stories to the forefront. Let us walk through the valleys of our experiences, knowing that even in the darkest moments, we are never truly alone. With God's grace and the support of one another, we can rise from the depths to the heights, discovering the richness of His love and the healing power that comes when we share our burdens with others.

Together, we will find hope that transcends our circumstances and rise, stronger, in faith.

CHAPTER 1

UNDERSTANDING DEPRESSION

Depression is a term that covers a wide spectrum of emotional states, ranging from mild sadness to profound despair. It is often marked by feelings of hopelessness, emptiness, and a loss of interest in activities that once brought joy. To utterly understand depression, one must recognize its complexity; it can be shaped by a variety of factors, including biological, psychological, and environmental influences. In my own life, I have experienced deep periods of depression, often triggered by significant losses. The grief of losing my mother and brother left me confused and overwhelmed by despair, making it nearly impossible to see beyond my pain. I found myself questioning my worth, my faith, and even the very purpose of my life. It was during these dark moments that I realized how vital it is to address depression openly, both for ourselves and for those who may be silently struggling. Many in the Christian community may find it difficult to reconcile their faith with feelings of depression. The belief that faith should shield us from suffering often leads to feelings of guilt and shame when those emotions surface. However, it is important to understand that even the most faithful individuals experience emotional struggles. Throughout the Bible, we see examples of great men and women who wrestled with despair such as David, who cried out in anguish in the Psalms, and Job, who questioned his suffering.

A common misconception is that depression signifies weak faith. This belief can create a barrier, preventing individuals from seeking help or even acknowledging their emotions.

It is essential to understand that experiencing depression does not diminish one's faith or relationship with God. Instead, it can be an opportunity for deeper reliance on Him and a more profound understanding of His grace. Throughout this chapter, I will examine various aspects of depression, including its

symptoms, misconceptions, and the importance of seeking help. I will also share insights from my journey, illustrating how acknowledging my struggles allowed me to find support and healing. By understanding depression holistically mind, body, and spirit we can begin to dismantle the stigma surrounding it and foster an environment of compassion and understanding.

Depression is not just a clinical diagnosis; it is a visceral experience that permeates every aspect of life. For me, its onset was gradual, creeping in like a fog after my mother passed away. I remember feeling an overwhelming heaviness as if I were carrying a weight that made even the simplest tasks seem insurmountable. I often withdrew from friends and family, avoiding social gatherings that had once brought me joy.

One particular evening stands out in my memory. I had been invited to a gathering at a friend's house for a chance to connect, laugh, and share stories. As I stood in front of the mirror, getting ready, I felt the familiar pull toward isolation. My heart raced, and my thoughts spiraled: What if they notice how sad I am? What if I cannot keep up with the conversation? Eventually, I canceled, choosing instead to stay home with my feelings, reinforcing the cycle of loneliness. This experience taught me just how debilitating depression can be not only emotionally but socially. The isolation compounded my grief, making it even harder to reach out for help. It was during these moments that I began to understand the importance of recognizing and confronting depression, not just within myself but in those around.

CHAPTER 2

BIBLICAL PERSPECTIVES ON DEPRESSION

The Bible is filled with accounts of individuals who faced deep sorrow and despair, reminding us that we are not alone in our struggles. From David's anguished cries to Jeremiah's profound lamentations, Scripture acknowledges the reality of human suffering and offers a pathway for expressing our pain.

David's Psalms are especially poignant in their raw honesty. In Psalm 42:11, he asks, "Why, my soul, are you downcast? Why so disturbed within me?" This question resonates deeply with those grappling with depression. It invites us to confront our feelings head-on rather than conceal them. David demonstrates the importance of lament, a practice often overlooked in contemporary worship but essential for processing grief and despair. Similarly, the story of Job serves as a powerful testament to the depth of human suffering. Job's life was upended, and he faced unimaginable loss. Yet despite his anguish, he remained honest with God about his emotions. In Job 30:20, he cries out, "I cry out to you, God, but you do not answer; I stand up, but you merely look at me." Job's story teaches us that it is okay to question, to feel anger, and to wrestle with our faith in times of distress.

In reflecting on these biblical accounts, we can glean valuable insights into our own struggles. They remind us that God does not turn away from our pain; rather, He invites us to bring our burdens before Him. This understanding dispels the myth that faith should shield us from sorrow. Instead, it is through vulnerability and honesty that we experience God's comfort and healing.

As we delve deeper into the biblical perspective on depression, we will explore how Scripture not only validates our feelings but also offers hope and guidance for navigating them. Through prayer, community, and a steadfast reliance on God's promises, we can find solace in our darkest moments and strengthen our faith in the process.

The Bible is rich with relatable accounts of suffering, and I found comfort in the stories of those who, like me, wrestled with despair. One of my favorites is the story of Elijah. After his monumental victory over the prophets of Baal, he fled in fear and found himself in a cave, crying out to God, "I've had enough, Lord!" **(1 Kings 19:4).** During my lowest moments, I deeply resonated with Elijah's sense of defeat. After unexpectedly losing my brother, I found myself asking

God similar questions: "Why is this happening?" "What have I done to deserve this?" In those times, I often turned to the Psalms, where David's raw emotions mirrored my own.

One night, I spent hours pouring out my heart in prayer, reading **Psalm 13:1-2:** "How long, O Lord? Will you forget me forever? How long will you hide your face from me?" I felt seen, as if David himself were sitting beside me in my anguish, reminding me that it is okay to cry out to God in our suffering.

CHAPTER 3
TRIALS AND SUFFERING

Every journey through depression is marked by trials that test our faith and resilience. My own experiences have been punctuated by moments of profound grief, particularly following the losses of my mother and brother. These events left indelible marks on my heart and soul, prompting me to confront the reality of suffering in ways I had never anticipated.

The Bible speaks extensively about suffering, emphasizing that it is a universal human experience. In **Romans 5:3-4,** Paul writes, "Not only so, but we also glory in our sufferings, because we know that suffering produces perseverance; perseverance, character; and character, hope." This passage encapsulates the idea that trials can lead to spiritual growth and deeper faith. However, when we find ourselves suffering, it can be challenging to see the path forward.

During my darkest moments, I often felt isolated and alone, questioning why I had to endure such pain. I grappled with feelings of inadequacy and doubt, wondering if I had somehow failed in my faith. Yet it was through this struggle that I discovered the importance of seeking God's presence. In my despair, I learned to lean into my faith rather than away from it. I began to find solace in prayer and Scripture, allowing God's promises to gradually restore my hope.

Throughout Scripture, we find examples of individuals who faced significant trials yet emerged with strengthened faith. Joseph, for instance, endured betrayal, imprisonment, and loneliness, yet he remained faithful to God. His story teaches us that even when circumstances seem dire, God is at work, orchestrating a greater purpose. As we reflect on the trials we face, it is essential to remember that our suffering does not define us; rather, it is a part of our journey toward deeper understanding and compassion. By embracing our pain and seeking God's presence within it, we can find the strength and resilience that empower us to help others who are struggling. The trial of losing my mother was transformative. I remember the day vividly: the phone call that shattered my world, the surreal moments that followed, and the overwhelming waves of grief that crashed over me. I felt as though I was walking through a dream, disconnected from reality. In the days that followed her passing, I struggled to make sense of it all. At times, I questioned my faith: Was God incredibly good if He allowed this to happen? Yet, in my despair, I also discovered the support of my faith community. A close friend, aware of my heartache, reached out and invited me to join a small group focused on healing. Reluctantly, I agreed. What if there was a safe space to share my pain and hear the stories of others? One woman, who had lost her husband, shared how her faith was tested but ultimately deepened through her grief. Her testimony gave me hope, showing me that it is possible to emerge from suffering with a renewed sense of purpose.

PERSONAL REFLECTIONS

13

"After the loss of my brother, I remember standing at his grave, grappling with the weight of my grief. It felt like the earth had been pulled from beneath me. I recalled David's words in Psalm 34:18: 'The Lord is close to the brokenhearted and saves those who are crushed in spirit.' This verse became a beacon of hope for me during those dark days."

Reflect on a time when you felt God's presence in your suffering. How did that experience shape your faith? Write about a specific moment of despair. What thoughts or feelings did you experience, and how did you respond?

CHAPTER 4

GOD'S PRESENCE IN DARKNESS

In moments of profound despair, it can feel as though God is distant as if our cries for help are met with silence. This feeling of abandonment can intensify the pain of depression, leading us to question our faith and self-worth. However, it is in these very moments that we must remind ourselves of the truth of Scripture: God is always present, even when we cannot feel Him.

My journey through grief often felt like navigating an impenetrable fog. There were times when I cried out to God, feeling as though my prayers were falling on deaf ears. In those moments, I struggled to understand why I felt so alone, even amidst my faith community. It was during this period of darkness that I discovered the importance of vulnerability and honesty in my prayers. I learned to express my feelings of abandonment to God, allowing myself to be genuine in my communication with Him. In Psalm 139:7-10, David reminds us, "Where can I go from your Spirit? Where can I flee from your presence? If I go up to the heavens, you are there; if I make my bed in the depths, you are there." These verses assure us that no matter how distant we may feel from God, He is always present, ready to embrace us in our pain. This truth became a lifeline for me as I sought comfort in my darkest hours.

Moreover, God's presence often manifests through the loving support of others. During my struggles, I found solace in the community of believers surrounding me. Friends and fellow missionaries offered their unwavering support, reminding me that I was not alone on my journey. Their encouragement served as a tangible expression of God's love and presence in my life. As we explore the theme of God's presence in darkness, we will examine practical ways to seek Him during our lowest points. Through prayer, Scripture meditation, and the support of our community, we can cultivate a deeper awareness of His abiding presence. By leaning into our faith, we can find the strength to face our struggles and the hope to rise from despair.

The feeling of God's absence can be suffocating, especially when we need Him the most. One particular night, after an exhausting week of work and grief, I sat on my bed, tears streaming down my face. I felt utterly alone, my prayers echoing in silence. At that moment, I reached for my Bible and opened it to Psalm 34:18: "The Lord is close to the brokenhearted and saves those who are crushed in spirit." As I read those words, a flicker of hope ignited within me. I began to realize that even in my despair, God was present though I often struggled to feel His presence.

The next day, I decided to visit my local church for a service. As I entered, I was enveloped by the warmth of the community. During worship, an unexpected sense of peace washed over me, as if God were gently reminding me that He had not abandoned me, even when my feelings suggested otherwise.

BIBLICAL VERSES AND REFLECTIONS

"Isaiah 41:10 says, 'So do not fear, for I am with you; do not be dismayed, for I am your God. I will strengthen you and help you; I will uphold you with my righteous right hand.' This verse reassured me during times when fear and anxiety threatened to overtake me."

CHAPTER 5

THE ROLE OF FAITH IN HEALING

Faith plays a pivotal role in the healing process, offering a foundation of hope and resilience amid life's storms. For many, it serves as a source of strength to navigate the complexities of depression and mental health. However, it is essential to understand that faith does not negate the reality of our struggles; rather, it complements our journey toward healing.

Throughout my life, I have witnessed the transformative power of faith in my healing. After experiencing profound loss, I initially struggled to reconcile my faith with my feelings of despair. Yet, as I began to turn to Scripture and prayer, I discovered that my faith could be a source of comfort rather than a barrier to my healing. In 1 Peter 5:7, we are encouraged to "cast all your anxiety on him because he cares for you." This verse reminds us that we are invited to bring our burdens before God, trusting in His care and compassion. Through this act of surrender, I began to experience healing by allowing myself to be vulnerable with God and acknowledging my pain.

Faith also fosters a sense of community, providing a crucial support network for healing. Engaging with fellow believers who understand the complexities of mental health can offer both comfort and encouragement. I found that sharing my struggles with trusted friends enabled me to process my feelings and receive prayerful support. Their presence reminded me that I was not alone, and their encouragement served as a testament to God's faithfulness. As we explore the role of faith in healing, we will delve into practical steps for nurturing our spiritual well-being. This includes cultivating a consistent prayer life, engaging with Scripture, and seeking community support. By actively integrating our faith into our healing journey, we can find the hope and strength to rise above our struggles.

Faith became my anchor during my darkest days, but it was not an easy journey. In the aftermath of my losses, I struggled with doubt and confusion. Yet, I realized that embracing my faith did not mean pretending to be okay; it was about being honest with God. I remember attending a retreat focused on healing, where participants shared their testimonies. One woman spoke of how her faith had been a refuge during her battle with depression. Her vulnerability inspired me to share my struggles. As I opened up about my grief, I felt a weight lift. In that moment, I understood that faith is not just about believing but also about expressing our deepest fears and doubts.

One night, I sat with my journal and penned a letter to God, pouring out my heart. I expressed my anger, confusion, and longing for understanding. The act of writing felt cathartic, a tangible release of emotions that had been bottled up inside. It was a significant step toward healing, reminding me that God welcomes our honesty.

STRATEGIES FOR DAILY LIVING

21

"Practical Steps Toward Healing"

"Consider developing a daily routine that includes:

Morning Prayer: Start each day with a prayer, asking God to guide you.

Gratitude Journaling: Write down three things you are grateful for each day to shift your focus toward positivity."

CHAPTER 6

THE COMFORT OF THE HOLY SPIRIT

The Holy Spirit is often called the Comforter, a guiding presence that brings solace and strength in times of need. Understanding the role of the Holy Spirit in our lives is crucial for navigating the challenges of depression. In moments of deep despair, the Holy Spirit offers comfort, reminding us of God's promises and rekindling hope in our hearts.

During my journey through depression, I experienced the profound comfort of the Holy Spirit in many ways. There were moments when I was overwhelmed by my emotions, but during prayer and reflection, I felt a gentle whisper assuring me that I was never alone. This divine comfort enabled me to lean into my faith rather than withdraw from it. In John 14:26, Jesus promises that the Holy Spirit will "teach you all things and remind you of everything I have said to you." This assurance is powerful for those struggling with depression, reminding us that we have a constant source of guidance and support. When we feel lost or overwhelmed, the Holy Spirit reminds us of God's truths and helps us find our way back to hope Beyond providing comfort, the Holy Spirit empowers us to take practical steps toward healing. Through inspiration and conviction, the Holy Spirit encourages us to seek help, whether through counseling, medication, or community support

Recognizing the Holy Spirit's role in our journey enables us to embrace healing as a holistic process one that integrates mind, body, and spirit. As we explore the comfort of the Holy Spirit, we will discuss how to cultivate a deeper relationship with Him through prayer, meditation, and studying Scripture.

By inviting the Holy Spirit into our healing journey, we can find strength to face our struggles and comfort in the assurance of God's presence. Experiencing the comfort of the Holy Spirit has been a transformative part of my healing. There were nights when I felt so overwhelmed that words escaped me. On one of those nights, I sat in silence, simply asking for peace. In that stillness, I felt an indescribable warmth enveloping me. It was as if a gentle presence assured me that I was not alone. In the days that followed, I began journaling more intentionally about my experiences, inviting the Holy Spirit into my reflections.

I also sought Scriptures that spoke of the Holy Spirit's comfort, like John 14:26, which reassured me that I had a Counselor who would remind me of God's truth. The more I leaned into this relationship, the more equipped I felt to face my struggles.

THE ROLE OF WORSHIP AND MUSIC

"Music became my solace during difficult times. Songs like 'What a Friend We Have in Jesus' reminded me that I could bring my burdens to Him. As I sang the lyrics, I felt a sense of peace wash over me, reinforcing the truth of Philippians 4:6-7: 'Do not be anxious about anything but in every situation, by prayer and petition, with thanksgiving, present your requests to God. And the peace of God, which transcends all understanding, will guard your hearts and your minds in Christ Jesus.'"

CHAPTER 7

BUILDING A SUPPORTIVE COMMUNITY

One of the most crucial aspects of navigating depression is the presence of a supportive community. As we journey through our struggles, the relationships we build can provide encouragement, understanding, and love. In my own experience, I have learned that we do not have to walk through our darkest moments alone; instead, we can lean on those around us for support.

During my time as a missionary, I witnessed the incredible power of community in the lives of those who were struggling. In various countries, I encountered individuals facing depression and other mental health challenges. What struck me most was the resilience that emerged when people came together to support one another. Whether through shared stories, prayer, or simply being present, these communities created safe spaces for individuals to express their struggles without fear of judgment. In Galatians 6:2, we are reminded to "carry each other's burdens, and in this way, you will fulfill the law of Christ." This call to bear one another's burdens is a beautiful reminder of the responsibility we have to support our fellow believers.

By creating environments where vulnerability is welcomed, we foster a sense of belonging and understanding. However, building a supportive community requires intentionality. It means reaching out to others, being willing to share our struggles, and being open to receiving help. In my journey, I learned the importance of vulnerability in relationships.

By sharing my experiences and seeking support, I discovered that many others were grappling with similar challenges. This mutual understanding became a source of strength, allowing us to walk alongside one another in our journeys. As we explore the importance of community, we will discuss practical steps for building supportive relationships. This includes finding accountability partners, participating in small groups, and engaging in meaningful conversations about mental health.

By fostering a culture of support within our faith communities, we can create an environment where individuals feel empowered to share their struggles and seek healing. Creating a supportive community became a lifeline in my journey. After my mother's passing, I hesitated to reach out to others, fearing I would burden them with my sorrow. But one day, a friend invited me to join a small group focused on prayer and support. Reluctantly, I attended, and what there was transformative.

Each person shared their struggles, creating an atmosphere of vulnerability and acceptance. One woman's story struck me deeply; she spoke about her battle with anxiety and how her faith community had been instrumental in her healing. Encouraged by her bravery, I shared my own experiences. As I spoke, I noticed nods of understanding around the room, reminding me that I was not alone in my journey. This sense of camaraderie became a source of strength. Together, we prayed for one another, supporting each other through the highs and lows.

CHAPTER 8
FINDING HOPE IN SCRIPTURE

Hope is a powerful force that can transform our perspective during times of despair. When we find ourselves overwhelmed by depression, it is essential to turn to Scripture for encouragement and reassurance. The Bible is filled with promises of hope that remind us of God's faithfulness and love, even in our darkest hours.

Throughout my journey, I have clung to verses that have provided strength and hope. For example, Jeremiah 29:11 reminds us that God has plans for us hope, and a future. In moments of doubt, this verse has served as a reminder that my life has a purpose, even when I cannot see the way forward.

Scripture also invites us to reflect on the character of God. In **Psalm 30:5**, we read, "Weeping may endure for a night, but joy comes in the morning." This verse encapsulates the promise that our current struggles are not the end of our story. God's faithfulness assures us that even in our darkest nights, morning will come.

As we explore the theme of hope in Scripture, we will delve into specific verses and passages that encourage. Each chapter will include reflection questions to help readers internalize these truths and apply them to their own lives. By meditating on God's Word, we can cultivate a mindset rooted in hope, allowing it to guide us through our struggles.

Additionally, we will discuss practical ways to incorporate Scripture into our daily lives. This may include memorizing verses, journaling reflections, and seeking accountability partners to share insights. By embedding hope into our spiritual practices, we can create a foundation of strength that sustains us during challenging times.

Scripture became a refuge for me during times of despair. One verse that particularly resonated with me was **Isaiah 41:10:** "Do not fear, for I am with you; do not be dismayed, for I am your God." During a particularly challenging week, I decided to write this verse on a sticky note and place it on my bathroom mirror.

Every morning, as I brushed my teeth, I would read those words and let them sink in. Slowly, they began to shift my perspective. Instead of focusing on my fear and sadness, I started to lean into the promise of God's presence.

One evening, I joined a small gathering with some of my young leaders to share our favorite Scriptures. As each of them read aloud, I could see the light in their eyes as they spoke about how certain verses had deeply resonated with their struggles. It was a powerful moment, as we experienced together how Scripture is alive and active, bringing comfort and hope when we need it most. This gathering became a reminder that, even in our hardest moments, God's Word continues to speak truth and healing into our lives.

CHAPTER 9

PRACTICAL STEPS TOWARD HEALING

Healing from depression is a journey that requires both spiritual and practical steps. While faith plays a vital role, it is equally important to recognize that healing often involves tangible actions and support. In my journey, I discovered that integrating practical strategies into my healing process allowed me to navigate my struggles more effectively.

One of the first steps I took was seeking professional help. Although this can be a daunting decision, reaching out to a counselor or therapist can provide invaluable support. They offer tools and strategies to help process feelings, identify triggers, and develop coping mechanisms. I found that talking to a professional not only validated my experiences but also equipped me with practical ways to manage my depression.

In addition to professional support, self-care practices became essential in my healing journey. This includes nurturing my physical, emotional, and spiritual well-being. Simple acts such as regular exercise, maintaining a healthy diet, and prioritizing sleep can significantly impact our mental health.

I learned that taking care of my body often helped lift my spirits, allowing me to feel more equipped to face challenges. Engaging in creative outlets, such as journaling and art, also played a crucial role in my healing. Writing became a therapeutic outlet for processing my emotions and reflecting on my experiences. Through journaling, I was able to articulate my thoughts and feelings, leading to a greater understanding of my journey.

As we explore practical steps toward healing, we will discuss various strategies that can support mental health. This includes developing healthy routines, practicing meditation, and seeking community involvement. By actively engaging in these practices, we can take ownership of our healing journey and cultivate resilience. Healing is not a linear journey; it requires intentional steps.

I learned the importance of developing a self-care routine that incorporated both spiritual and physical elements. One practical step I took was to create a daily schedule that included time for exercise, prayer, and journaling.

Even though I knew that reaching out to others would help me, I struggled to do so, which kept me isolated. I encourage you to find the strength to reach out; it can significantly aid your healing process. I discovered that this small change positively impacted my mood and energy levels.

Additionally, I committed to checking in with friends regularly by scheduling coffee dates or phone calls. These connections became a vital part of my healing journey, reminding me of the importance of community in overcoming isolation. Afterward, I would spend time in prayer, inviting God into my day and seeking His guidance.

TESTIMONIALS

35

"In a recent conversation with a friend, she shared how her faith sustained her during her battle with anxiety. 'I found that praying Scripture helped me anchor my thoughts and find peace,' she said. Her testimony highlights the power of community and shared faith in healing."

CHAPTER10

WRESTLING WITH DARKNESS

The Spiritual Battle in the Depression

Depression is more than just a feeling of sadness or discouragement it is often a deep, consuming darkness that can cloud our thoughts, distort our emotions, and make us feel utterly alone. It is a battle not just of the mind but of the spirit as well. For those who experience depression, the struggle can feel endless and overwhelming, as if they are sinking into an abyss with no hope of rescue.

But as believers, we must remember that depression is not just a psychological issue; it is also a spiritual battle. The Bible makes it clear that we live in a world where spiritual warfare is real. In **Ephesians 6:12,** Paul writes, "For our struggle is not against flesh and blood, but against the rulers, against the authorities, against the powers of this dark world and the spiritual forces of evil in the heavenly realms." Depression can sometimes be a manifestation of this battle, a fight for our hearts, our minds, and our faith.

One of the greatest lies that depression tells us is that we are alone that no one understands, and that God Himself has abandoned us. This is a tactic of the enemy, who seeks to isolate us from the truth of God's love and presence. But the truth is, even in our darkest moments, God is with us.

In **Psalm 139:7-12,** David beautifully expresses this reality:

"Where can I go from your Spirit?

Where can I flee from your presence?

If I go up to the heavens, you are there.

if I make my bed in the depths, you are there.

If I rise on the wings of the dawn,

if I settle on the far side of the sea,

even there your hand will guide me,

your right hand will hold me fast.

If I say, 'Surely the darkness will hide me.

and the light become night around me,'

even the darkness will not be dark to you.

the night will shine like the day,

for darkness is as light to you."

Amid depression, it can feel like the darkness is suffocating, like there is no way out. But even in the depths, God is there. He is present with us in our pain, and He is fighting for us, even when we cannot feel His presence. Our emotions might tell us one thing, but God's truth tells us another He has not abandoned us.

Understanding the Spiritual Roots of Depression

It is important to recognize that depression can have spiritual roots. In the Bible, we see many examples of faithful men and women of God who struggled with deep emotional pain, grief, and even despair. One of the clearest examples is the prophet, Elijah. In **1 Kings 19,** Elijah had just experienced a great victory over the prophets of Baal, yet soon after, he fled into the wilderness, overwhelmed with fear and exhaustion. He became so discouraged that he asked God to take his life, saying, "I have had enough, Lord. Take my life; I am no better than my ancestors" **(1 Kings 19:4).** Elijah was at the end of his rope, emotionally and spiritually drained. He felt utterly alone and believed his life had no more purpose.

But God did not leave Elijah in that place of despair. Instead, He met Elijah in his brokenness. He provided rest, nourishment, and eventually a fresh encounter with His presence. Elijah's story reminds us that even the mightiest servants of God can experience depression, but God's response is always one of compassion and restoration.

Depression can also be exacerbated by spiritual oppression. The enemy seeks to take advantage of our vulnerabilities, whispering lies into our hearts and minds. He tells us that we are worthless, that God does not care, and that there is no way out of the darkness. These are lies, plain and simple. **John 8:44** calls Satan the "father of lies," and one of his greatest weapons is deception. He knows how to twist the truth and manipulate our thoughts when we are at our weakest.

But the Bible also gives us the tools to combat these spiritual attacks. **Ephesians 6:10-18** speaks of the armor of God the belt of truth, the breastplate of righteousness, the shield of faith, the helmet of salvation, the sword of the Spirit (which is the Word of God), and prayer. When we feel overwhelmed by depression, we must turn to these spiritual defenses, reminding ourselves of God's truth and seeking His strength to fight the battle.

The Role of Scripture and Prayer in the Battle

One of the most powerful ways to fight against depression is by immersing ourselves in God's Word. The Bible is filled with promises of hope, comfort, and strength for those who are struggling. When we are in the midst of depression, it is easy to feel like those promises do not apply to us, but the truth is, they are meant for exactly those moments of pain and confusion.

Here are a few verses to meditate on when depression feels overwhelming: **Psalm 34:17-18:** "The righteous cry out, and the Lord hears them; he delivers them from all their troubles. The Lord is close to the brokenhearted and saves those who are crushed in spirit." **Isaiah 41:10:** "So do not fear, for I am with you; do not be dismayed, for I am your God. I will strengthen you and help you; I will uphold you with my righteous right hand." **Matthew 11:28-30:** "Come to me, all you who are weary and burdened, and I will give you rest. Take my yoke upon you and learn from me, for I am gentle and humble in heart, and you will find rest for your souls. For my yoke is easy and my burden is light."

In addition to Scripture, prayer is an essential tool in the spiritual battle of depression. Prayer allows us to bring our pain, confusion, and questions to God. We do not have to hide our feelings from Him, He already knows them. Like Elijah, we can pour out our hearts to God in honesty, and He will meet us with grace.

One of the most powerful prayers we can pray in the midst of depression is simply, "Help me, Lord." It does not have to be eloquent or long, just honest. God hears our cries, and He is near to the brokenhearted. **Romans 8:26** offers comfort in times when we do not even have the strength to pray: "In the same way, the Spirit helps us in our weakness. We do not know what we ought to pray for, but the Spirit himself intercedes for us through wordless groans." Even when we feel too weak to pray, the Holy Spirit is praying for us, lifting us up before the Father.

Finding Hope in the Midst of the Battle

The battle against depression is not one that we fight alone. God is with us, and He has equipped us with everything we need to stand firm. While the darkness may feel overwhelming at times, we can trust that God's light is stronger. John 1:5 says, "The light shines in the darkness, and the darkness has not overcome it."

It is also important to remember that depression is not a sign of spiritual failure or weakness. Many of God's greatest servants, from David to Elijah to the apostle Paul, experienced times of deep emotional and spiritual struggle. But God used them mightily, despite their battles.

In the same way, God can use your struggle with depression to bring you closer to Him, to deepen your faith, and to equip you to help others who are facing the same battle. As you lean on Him and fight this battle with His strength, He will bring you through to the other side.

No matter how deep the darkness may seem, remember that God's light will always break through. He is fighting for you, and He will never leave you alone.

CHAPTER 11

HOPE IN THE VALLEY

Overcoming Despair through Faith

There is a unique and profound pain that comes from walking through the valley of depression. It is a place where hope seems distant, the future feels uncertain, and each day seems to blend into the next with an overwhelming sense of heaviness. In this valley, despair can feel suffocating, isolating, and relentless. But the Bible gives us a powerful message for such times: we are not alone in the valley, and God's hope can sustain us, even in the deepest darkness.

When I reflect on my own journey through the valley of depression, I am reminded of moments when it felt like I was trudging through thick mud, with each step forward feeling harder than the last. I know what it is like to feel spiritually dry, emotionally exhausted, and physically drained. The valley is a place where even the smallest tasks getting out of bed, speaking to a friend, or reading a Bible verse can feel like monumental challenges.

But it is also in that valley where I learned something transformative: God does not abandon us in our despair. Instead, He walks with us, carrying us when we cannot carry ourselves, and whispering hope into the depths of our pain.

In **Psalm 23:4,** David writes, "Even though I walk through the darkest valley, I will fear no evil, for you are with me; your rod and your staff, they comfort me." This verse speaks directly to the experience of walking through the valley of depression. The "darkest valley" that David describes could easily be the place of mental and emotional despair, yet his declaration is bold he will not fear. Why? Because God is with him, offering comfort and guidance, even in the darkest places.

The Reality of the Valley

Let us be honest: walking through the valley is not easy. There is no quick fix or magic prayer that makes the heaviness of depression disappear overnight. When you are in the valley, it can feel endless. It can feel like God is far away, like your prayers are hitting a ceiling, or like you are losing the battle for your mind and heart.

In moments like this, it is important to remember that the valley is not a sign of spiritual failure. Many of the Bible's greatest heroes walked through dark valleys. Take David, for example. He was described as a man after God's own heart, yet he wrestled with despair and deep emotional pain. In **Psalm 42:11,** David asks, "Why, my soul, are you downcast? Why so disturbed within me?" This is not a man who has it all together this is someone who understands the weight of depression.

And David is not alone. Elijah, after defeating the prophets of Baal, fled into the wilderness, and told God that he wanted to **die (1 Kings 19).** Jeremiah, the "weeping prophet," lamented the day he was born **(Jeremiah 20:14-18).** Even Jesus, in the Garden of Gethsemane, was "overwhelmed with sorrow to the point of death" **(Matthew 26:38).**

Depression and despair are not foreign to the people of faith. They are part of the human experience in a broken world. But here is the powerful truth: while the valley is real, it is not permanent. The valley is a place we pass through, not a place we stay. As David wrote, "Even though I walk through the darkest valley…" he did not set up camp there. He did not resign himself to living in despair forever. He kept walking, trusting that God would lead him through.

God's Presence in the Depths

One of the hardest parts of depression is the feeling of abandonment or isolation. The enemy often uses depression to convince us that we are alone, that no one understands what we are going through, and that even God has turned His back on us. But that is not true. In **Psalm 139:7-12,** David writes, "Where can I go from your Spirit? Where can I flee from your presence? If I go up to the heavens, you are there; if I make my bed in the depths, you are there." This passage reminds us that there is nowhere we can go where God is not present. Even when we feel like we are in the depths emotionally, mentally, or spiritually God is there with us. When depression tells us that we are alone, we have to fight back with the truth of God's Word: He is with us. He sees us in our pain, He hears our cries, and He cares deeply about what we are going through. **Hebrews 4:15** tells us that Jesus can sympathize with our weaknesses because He experienced every form of suffering, including emotional anguish. In the Garden of Gethsemane, Jesus prayed so intensely that His sweat became like drops of blood **(Luke 22:44).** He understands the weight of deep sorrow, and He walks with us through it.

The Journey of Hope

Hope may seem like an abstract concept when you are in the valley, but the Bible speaks of hope as something that is living and active. **1**

Peter 1:3 says, "Praise be to the God and Father of our Lord Jesus Christ! In his great mercy, he has given us new birth into a living hope through the resurrection of Jesus Christ from the dead." Our hope is not based on wishful thinking or positive affirmations it is anchored in the person of Jesus Christ.

One of the biggest turning points in my battle with depression came when I realized that hope was not something I had to manufacture on my own. It was not about me trying to feel better or "fix" myself. Hope was something that God was offering to me, even when I felt hopeless.

It is important to understand that hope is not about denying the reality of our pain. Hope does not mean pretending that everything is fine or forcing a smile when we feel like we are falling apart. True hope acknowledges the depth of our struggle while also believing that God is bigger than our despair. **Romans 8:24-25** says, "For in this hope we were saved. But hope that is seen is no hope at all. Who hopes for what they already have? But if we hope for what we do not yet have, we wait for it patiently."

This verse speaks to the tension we often feel in the valley we are waiting for the fullness of God's healing, for the day when all things will be made new. In the meantime, we hold onto hope, even when we cannot see the full picture.

Practical Steps to Cultivate Hope

When you are in the valley of depression, hope can feel like a flickering flame, easily extinguished by the winds of despair. But just as you protect a candle from being blown out, there are practical steps we can take to guard and nurture hope in our lives.

Cling to God's Word.

The Bible is filled with promises of hope, comfort, and strength. Even when it is hard to read or when the words feel distant, make a habit of immersing yourself in Scripture. Write down verses that speak to your heart and place them where you can see them daily. Some powerful verses include **Psalm 34:17-18:** "The righteous cry out, and the Lord hears them; he delivers them from all their troubles. The Lord is close to the brokenhearted and saves those who are crushed in spirit." **Isaiah 41:10:** "So do not fear, for I am with you; do not be dismayed, for I am your God. I will strengthen you and help you; I will uphold you with my righteous right hand." **Matthew 11:28-30:** "Come to me, all you who are weary and burdened, and I will give you rest. Take my yoke upon you and learn from me, for I am gentle and humble in heart, and you will find rest for your souls. For my yoke is easy and my burden is light."

Pray, even when it is hard.

Prayer does not always have to be eloquent or long. Sometimes, the most powerful prayer you can pray in the valley is, "Help me, Lord." God hears every cry of our hearts, and He is always listening. **Romans 8:26** tells us that when we do not know what to pray, the Holy Spirit intercedes for us with groanings too deep for words. Even when we do not have the strength to pray, the Spirit is praying on our behalf.

Surround yourself with a community.

One of the enemy's tactics is to isolate us in the valley, making us believe that we have to face depression alone. But God created us for the community. Find people who can walk with you through the valley whether it is a trusted friend, a pastor, or a counselor. Let them pray for you, encourage you, and remind you of God's faithfulness when you are struggling to see it yourself.

Embrace small steps of healing.

When you are in the depths of depression, even small acts of self-care can feel overwhelming. But healing often happens in small, gradual steps. Whether it is taking a walk, journaling your thoughts, or simply getting out of bed in the morning, each step is a victory. Celebrate the small moments of progress, knowing that God is walking with you every step of the way.

A Future Filled with Hope

The valley may be dark, but it is not your final destination. God has promised a future filled with hope for those who trust in Him. **Jeremiah 29:11** says, "For I know the plans I have for you," declares the Lord, "plans to prosper you and not to harm you, plans to give you hope and a future." This verse is not just for people whose lives are going well it is for those in the valley, too.

God's plans for your life are good, even when you cannot see the way forward. The valley is not where your story ends. Keep walking, keep trusting, and keep holding onto the hope that God is with you, guiding you through every step.

REFLECTION VERSE:

50

"Even though I walk through the darkest valley, I will fear no evil, for you are with me; your rod and your staff, they comfort me." **Psalm 23:4 (NIV)**

REFLECTION

51

As you reflect on this chapter, think about the valleys you have walked through in your own life. How has God shown His presence to you, even in the darkest times? What are some practical ways you can cultivate hope, even when the road ahead feels uncertain?

PRAYER

52

Dear God,

Thank You for being with me in the valley. Help me to remember that I am not alone and that You are walking with me, even in the darkest moments. Give me the strength to keep trusting You, and the hope to believe that better days are ahead. Help me to cling to Your promises and to find comfort in Your presence. Thank You for Your unfailing love and for the future You have prepared for me. Amen.

CHAPTER 12

CELEBRATING GOD'S FAITHFULNESS

As we reach the final chapter of this journey, it is essential to take a moment to celebrate God's faithfulness. Throughout my experiences with depression, I have witnessed the profound ways in which God has walked alongside me. Each step of the journey, though filled with challenges, has been marked by His unwavering love and support.

In Psalm 136, we read the refrain, "His love endures forever." This reminder of God's enduring love is a powerful affirmation of His faithfulness in our lives. Despite the trials we face, we can find solace in the knowledge that God is always present, working all things together for our good (Romans 8:28). Celebrating God's faithfulness also involves recognizing the progress we have made in our healing journey. While it is easy to focus on the challenges we face, it is equally important to acknowledge the victories no matter how small. Whether it is finding hope in a difficult situation, reaching out for help, or experiencing moments of joy, these milestones are worthy of celebration.

As we conclude this book, I encourage you to reflect on your own journey. Take time to celebrate the ways in which God has been faithful in your life. This may involve journaling about your experiences, sharing your story with others, or simply taking a moment to express gratitude. In closing, I want to remind you that you are not alone in your struggles. As we journey together from the depths to the heights, let us continue to seek God's presence, rely on the comfort of the Holy Spirit, and support one another in our healing journeys. May we emerge from our trials with a deeper understanding of God's love and an unwavering hope for the future. As I reflect on my journey, I am reminded of the countless ways God has shown His faithfulness. Each step I took toward healing, each prayer, each conversation, and each moment of vulnerability was met with grace. One of the most poignant moments of celebration came during a worship service at my church. As we sang a song about God's goodness, I was overwhelmed with gratitude. It was a profound realization that, despite my struggles, I had emerged with a deeper faith and a renewed sense of purpose.

Though I did not have anyone to celebrate with, I took the time to reflect on my journey and the progress I had made. I wrote down stories of hope and moments of growth, reminding myself of how I had become stronger through my trials. This reflection served as a powerful reminder that, even in our darkest moments, God is weaving a beautiful story of redemption and healing.

Navigating Depression

Common Questions of Faith

Is it wrong to feel depressed as a believer?

Many people struggle with the belief that their faith should protect them from feelings of depression. It is important to understand that experiencing depression does not mean a lack of faith. Numerous biblical figures, like David and Elijah, openly expressed their anguish.

How can I reconcile my faith with feelings of despair?

It is essential to recognize that feelings of despair are part of the human condition. Honest prayer and reflection can help you bridge the gap between faith and emotion.

Does God still love me when I feel this way?

Absolutely! God's love is unconditional, and nothing can separate you from His love (Romans 8:38-39). Your feelings do not determine your worth in His eyes.

Should I seek professional help or just rely on prayer?

Seeking professional help is both a valid and wise choice. While prayer is important, professional support can offer additional tools for healing.

How can I find comfort in Scripture during dark times?

Seek out verses that speak to your heart. Writing them down, memorizing them, or meditating on them can help instill hope and encouragement.

What role does the community play in my healing?

Community plays a crucial role. Surrounding yourself with supportive friends and family can offer encouragement, understanding, and a safe space to share your struggles.

ENCOURAGEMENT TO OTHERS

58

"To those supporting loved ones with depression: Remember to listen actively and offer compassion without judgment. Proverbs 17:17 states, 'A friend loves at all times, and a brother is born for a time of adversity.' Your presence can be a source of strength."

REFLECTION ON HOPE AND RECOVERY

"As I reflect on my journey, I hold onto the promise of Jeremiah 29:11: 'For I know the plans I have for you,' declares the Lord, 'plans to prosper you and not to harm you, plans to give you hope and a future.' This assurance has been a guiding light, reminding me that healing is a process filled with purpose."

INVITATION FOR INTERACTION

60

"I invite you to share your story. Whether through email, social media, or a dedicated website, your experiences can help others feel less alone. Together, we can build a community of hope and support."

A Prayer for Healing and Hope

Heavenly Father,

In moments of darkness and despair, I come before You with a heavy heart. I ask for Your comfort and peace to envelop me. Help me to remember that You are always with me, even when I feel alone. Lord, grant me the courage to face my feelings and to seek help when needed. May Your Holy Spirit guide me through this journey of healing, reminding me of Your promises and unfailing love. I pray for the strength to reach out to others, to share my burdens, and to find solace in the community. Thank You for the hope that You offer, even amid my struggles. As I navigate this path, may I lean on You for support and wisdom. Help me to trust in Your plan for my life and to find joy in the little things each day. In Jesus' name, I pray. Amen.

HOW TO SEEK AND FIND HELP

Seeking Help: Steps Toward Healing

- Acknowledge Your Feelings: The first step is recognizing that you are struggling and that it is okay to seek help. Validate your emotions and remember that you are not alone.

- Reach Out to Trusted Friends or Family: Share your struggles with someone you trust. Opening up can bring relief and lead to supportive conversations.

- Engage with Your Faith Community: Many churches offer resources for mental health support, including counseling or support groups. Do not hesitate to reach out to your church leaders.

- Consult a Mental Health Professional: Consider seeking a counselor or therapist who specializes in mental health. Professional support can provide you with tools and strategies tailored to your specific needs.

- Utilize Hotlines and Resources: Many organizations offer hotlines and resources for those dealing with mental health challenges. Keep these numbers nearby for immediate support.

- Practice Self-Care: Integrate self-care practices into your daily routine, such as exercise, healthy eating, journaling, or engaging in hobbies that bring you joy.

- Pray and Meditate: Lean on your faith through prayer and meditation. These practices can help center your thoughts and bring peace in difficult times.

By taking these steps, you can move toward healing and find the support you need on your journey.

CONCLUSION

Thank you for joining me on this journey through the complexities of depression from a biblical perspective. I hope that this exploration has offered you insights, encouragement, and practical tools to help you navigate your struggles. Remember, healing is a journey, one we do not have to walk alone. As we continue to seek God's presence, embrace vulnerability, and support one another, we can find hope and strength to rise from the depths into the heights of faith.

INDEX

A

- Abandonment, feelings of, Chapter 4
- Acknowledgments, 2
- Anxiety, coping with, Chapter 9
- Acceptance, the journey of, Chapter 10
- Accountability, the role of, Chapter 7

B

- Biblical perspectives on depression, Chapter 2
- Biblical figures who suffered.
  - David, Chapter 2
  - Job, Chapter 2
  - Elijah, Chapter 2
- Biblical verses
  - Isaiah 41:10, Chapter 4
  - Jeremiah 29:11, Chapter 10
  - Philippians 4:6-7, Chapter 5
  - Romans 5:3-4, Chapter 6
  - Psalm 34:18, Chapter 3
  - Psalm 13:1-2, Chapter 2
  - 1 Peter 5:7, Chapter 5

C

- Comfort of the Holy Spirit, Chapter 6
- Community support, Chapter 7
- Coping mechanisms, Chapter 9
- Counseling, seeking professional help, Chapter 9

D

- Depression
  - Definition and understanding, Chapter 1
  - Questions of faith, Chapter 12
  - Personal experiences with, throughout the book

E

- Encouragement to others, Chapter 10
- Emotional expression, biblical examples of, Chapter2
- Experiences, and personal reflections, throughout the book

F

- Faith and healing, Chapter 5
- Faith practices, Chapter 5
- Forgiveness, role of in healing, Chapter 10

G

- Guided journaling prompts, Appendix

H

- Hope
  - Finding in Scripture, Chapter 8
  - Recovery, Chapter 10
  - Personal testimonies of Chapter 10

I

- Invitation for interaction, 13
- Isolation, effects of, Chapter 1

J

- Journaling, benefits of, Chapter 9

M

- Mental health resources, Appendix
- Music as a comfort, Chapter 6

P

- Prayer for healing, 13
- Practical resources for support, Appendix
- Practical steps toward healing, Chapter 9
- Purpose in suffering, Chapter 10

R

- Reflection questions, Appendix
- Resilience, building, Chapter 9

S

- Scripture references
- Self-care practices, Chapter 9
- Support resources, Appendix.
- Spiritual growth through trials, Chapter 3

T

- Trials and suffering, Chapter 3
- The role of worship and music, Chapters 5 & 6
- Theological insights, Chapter 2

W

- Worship practices, Chapter 5

CALL TO ACTION

As we come to the close of this journey together, I want to encourage you to take the next steps in your healing process. If you are struggling with depression, know that you are not alone. Many have walked this path before you, and there is hope for brighter days ahead.

- Reach Out for Support: Do not hesitate to seek help from friends, family, or a mental health professional. Sharing your struggles can be a powerful first step toward healing. Remember, it is okay to ask for help.

- Engage with Your Faith Community: Connect with others who share your faith. Whether it is joining a small group, attending a church service, or participating in prayer meetings, being surrounded by supportive people can provide immense comfort.

- Incorporate Spiritual Practices: Make prayer and Scripture reading a daily habit. Turn to verses that resonate with your heart and let them remind you of God's love and faithfulness.

- Practice Self-Care: Prioritize your physical and emotional well-being. Incorporate activities that bring you joy, whether it is exercise, hobbies, or spending time in nature. Your mental health matters.

- Share Your Story: Consider sharing your experiences with others. Your journey can inspire and uplift those who may be struggling in silence. Together, we can break the stigma surrounding mental health.

- Stay Open to Healing: Healing is a journey that takes time. Be patient with yourself and trust that every step forward, no matter how small, is a victory.

- Join a Support Group: Look for local or online support groups where you can connect with others facing similar challenges. Sharing experiences and coping strategies can foster a sense of community and belonging.

As you move forward, hold onto the truth that God is with you every step of the way. His love endures forever, and His promises are a source of hope and strength. I invite you to take these steps and embrace the journey toward healing. Your story is not over there is more to come, and brighter days are ahead. Together, let us rise from the depths to the heights of faith and hope.